Mentoring Startups Entrepreneurs

Lessons I learnt from Success and Failures

Dhananjaya Parkhe

1st Edition

Introduction to Mentoring Startups Entrepreneurs — 3
Getting Started- Cheer Up! — 5
Who is an Entrepreneur — 7
Definition — 7
The Cornerstones of Successful Internet Entrepreneurship — 8
Why so many Internet Startups Fail? — 8
Skills? Employment? Or Entrepreneur? — 13
Sharing an Inspiring Story, I recently read — 13
Own/Borrowed investment? — 17
Self-Investment Tips — 17
You Like Work or Making Deals? — 20
Why does your Startups need a Mentor? — 26
How a Mentor helps? — 26
Startup Founder vs Entrepreneur — 30
Differences in Goals — 30
How I became a Mentor? — 34

Introduction to Mentoring Startups Entrepreneurs

We lived in Bhopal the State Capital of a Newly carved state in 1958. My father was a Government servant and mother a housewife. She has passed Intermediate and was trained Montessori Teacher but had never practiced.

She and her friend Tai Nafde found a need in the new township of T.T. Nagar for a kindergarten / pre-school / play school cum crèche' in this developing cosmopolitan suburb full of Government employees transferred from Maharashtra, UP, Bihar, Southern Bengaluru.

The Old town had its own system of education and there were developed systems. The two ladies spoke to neighborhood and decided to start a 'BALAK MANDIR' – initially a playschool cum crèche' and slowly began admitting students for nursery and kindergarten. They had just about 30 kids to begin with. The timings were from 10 AM till 5pm and if parents wished to take kids home early they were flexible.

The fees were nominal INR 2 per month which was affordable and they did not provide any food or milk/ vegetables – it was to be provided by the parents.

This was our first experience of Entrepreneurship. I was 5 years of age and was preparing to go to the school when this venture started. It worked very well and began getting famous and growing so much so that my mother and her friend both began running independent Balak Mandirs or today's Play Schools at their own homes and the demand was still growing.

One day, my aunt who was a Director of Tribal Welfare landed into our home with her beautiful smart looking lady friend who arrived in a long Impala (Chevrolet) or something like that of a car I remember it was open hood and very long with a chauffeur). They discussed with my mom and her friend for an hour and by evening my mother decided to give up the Balak Mandir to her friend as she was Offered a Job in the Government's Education Department as a Teacher for Kindergarten project which the State was starting. The lady was Director of Public Instructions DPI as she was called – was an ex-Royal from Bhopal family and a powerful persona.

This was my earliest memory and inception into Entrepreneurship. My mother continued in Government service and post retirement worked for

Vanvasi Kalyan Ashram and Shabri Kanya Ashram in Raipur and interior Chhattisgarh teaching small children till the end. That was her mission and purpose of life and she dedicated it for the cause. I met several girls from age 2 -22 in her hostel who were mainly from Northeast and my mom was their Didi/ Teacher/ friend/ philosopher and guide.

The mother's friend continued with her Balak Mandir and did it without many expansions – she was content having a batch of 30-35 children which she could manage with the help of two young teachers/ help. She also did it for many years.

No financial help from anyone, much to the chagrin of my father and uncle (my mother's; friends husband the two ladies decided a course – and became successful entrepreneurs. They also helped many ladies to start similar outfits in other localities as mentors free of charge.

I learnt my second lesson – Mentoring is Free. I am happy to share some of my successes and failures in my efforts of Starting Up trying to be an Entrepreneur here. I hope they are useful for the Startups Entrepreneurs of this Generation.

Getting Started- Cheer Up!

There is no wine if Grapes are not Pressed

No Perfume if Flowers are not Crushed

If you feel any Pressures in life,

It means God is Bringing the Best out of You.

Chapter Number 1
Who is an Entrepreneur
Definition

from Dictionary.com.

Merriam-Webster: "one who organizes, manages and assumes the risks of a business or enterprise."

Dictionary.com: "a person who organizes and manages any enterprise, especially a business, usually with considerable initiative and risk.

The Key words to learn from Merriam Webster definition are:

Organizing
Managing
Risk Assumption
Risk Bearing ability
Running a Business Enterprise.

From the Dictionary definition, the Learnings also are:

Managing Business
Managing an Enterprise
Considerable Initiative and
Risk Taking

also implied are what I called as 'Finishiative' - The Drive and passion which makes an Entrepreneur to go for the Finish line like in a Marathon Race Runner!

Chapter Number 2

The Cornerstones of Successful Internet Entrepreneurship

Why so many Internet Startups Fail?

Running a successful internet business can look so simple when you are on the outside looking in. You look at a successful internet entrepreneur and he doesn't look like he is doing anything special but he is living the good life. It doesn't look like he is working all that hard. He seems to be enjoying life immensely.

Really. all he is doing is sitting comfortably in front of his own computer in his own very comfortable home a few hours a day. He talks on the telephone and seems to be enjoying every conversation.

Apparently, running a successful internet business is the proverbial 'piece of cake'! Right? WRONG!!! Wrong, wrong, wrong!

You are looking at the results of a very, very long and tedious process that consisted of many very long, late-night hours and a lot of blood, sweat and tears over a period of several years.

This successful internet entrepreneur worked very, very hard for the success that you are looking at.

It is more than a little bit likely that he first placed four corner stone's first as he began the long process of building his successful Internet business. Those four corner stones upon which he built his success are:

The right mind set.

Recognizing and using leverage.

Building a set of useful contacts.

And he probably had a mentor.

We will discuss these four corner stones that must be laid down first so that a successful internet business can be constructed.

All of them are important, even crucial to the success of any business but especially to the success of an internet based business.

Constructing a successful business in cyber space has many things in common with the building of a successful brick and mortar business but there are significant differences as well.

Having the Right, Healthy Mindset

The success of any business both online variety as well as the off-line variety require the right mindset from the get-go.

A right and healthy mind set will not guarantee success but a wrong and unhealthy or unrealistic mindset will most assuredly guarantee failure. So, the right mind set is the first corner stone that must be laid upon which a successful business can be constructed.

What is a right and healthy mindset? There are things that it is as well as things that it isn't.

A right and healthy mindset IS the willingness to work as hard and if is necessary to achieve the goals that has been set. A right and healthy mindset ISN'T the belief that success will be easy, quick or painless.

Those who believe that they can make an internet business enterprise thrive without having to put in any time or effort are simply doomed to failure from the beginning.

There are schemers and scammers out there in cyberspace that are just waiting eagerly for those to come along who are looking for easy riches.

A right and healthy mindset IS the willingness to take the time to make a good, solid business plan that is based upon sound business principles.

A right and healthy mindset ISN'T just jumping in feet first and hoping for the best. The best that can happen under those circumstances is that you get out with any more than two cents to your name.

'Flying by the seat of your pants' is NOT a plan…it is just plain suicide in the world of internet marketing. If you don't have a formal education in business, you need to find people who do have that kind of education and seek then follow their advice.

Recognizing and Using Leverage

There are dozens…maybe hundreds…. of business models, out there. Some are, of course, more successful than others but they all come with their own set of pros and cons.

The idea is to get the most bang for the buck. You need to use all the power of the Internet to make your e-business successful. You cannot afford to leave any stone unturned.

If you are a real go-getter, the temptation is to do everything first and that isn't possible. You need to make a realistic plan and build one thing upon another until you have a good solid base from which to operate.

Once you get a website built, you will need to begin leveraging SEO (search engine optimization) and gaining page rank.

One thing does lead to another, of course, but one of the quickest ways to leverage SEO is to add a blog to your website. This is a way that you can get much more quickly indexed by the search engines.

Leveraging also includes branding yourself, your website and your products. One of the quicker ways to begin to get yourself branded is by investing in

PLR (Private Label Rights) products and changing the names of those products to include your own name or logo. (Don't forget that there must be some rewriting done.)

This is probably the quickest way to become branded as well as gain credibility on the internet. For example: you might by a PLR E-Book about Easy Dog Training and change the name to 'John Doe's Easy Dog Training Methods'.

You can sell the book, give it away as a gift on your own website or list it in E-Book repositories for others to use.

Remember that reputation and credibility are everything on the internet. Don't take any shortcuts and never damage or allow others to damage either.

It Is Not What You Know, But Who You Know

That is an old saying. "It is not What you know, but Who you know that counts". Setting a corner stone of good solid relationships is an important aspect of building a successful e-enterprise.

Working hard at building good solid business relationships is worth every minute of time that you invest in it. Business relationship building should be one of your top priorities.

When you build social relationships, you insert yourself into social situations where you meet people who have interests that are like or complimentary to your own interests don't you?

That is precisely the same way that business relationships are established. You insert yourself into business situations where you will meet others who have businesses that are like or complimentary to your own business. You develop relationships over a period.

There are several ways in which to accomplish this task. One way is to participate in teleseminars or webinars that are related to your business.

You will learn a lot, of course, but equally important, you will meet those who are already succeeding in the niche market that you are working in.

Of course, attending real brick and mortar world seminars is an even better way to begin to build friendly business relationships with not only your peers but also with those who can help you.... which brings me to the final corner stone that you need to lay.

Find a Capable Mentor

It isn't likely that there is a more asset that a new e-entrepreneur can have than a good and capable mentor. Someone who has already made all the mistakes can help you to avoid making all the mistakes yourself.

They have the wisdom that comes from experience to point out pitfalls and to help direct you toward the better of choices.

Why, you ask, would anyone who has it made want to take their time to help a newbie succeed?

Maybe I can answer that by telling you about my friend who is an accomplished musician. He played with some of the biggest stars in the business. He is a very, very fine guitarist who is now in his 70's.

He has about three young guitarists that he spends many hours not only teaching how to play but counseling them on career choices.

I asked him why he spent so much time doing that and he said, "It is like gaining immortality. If I teach them and they teach others, then what I know lives forever."

Successful internet marketers want that 'immortality' as well. The ones who are the very most successful are the ones, amazingly enough, who are the most likely to mentor an up and coming e-entrepreneur.

Of course, these successful internet marketers are not going to be interested in wasting their time on a person who has not already worked hard to lay those first three corner stone's themselves.

These potential mentors are looking for new comers who show that they have a right and healthy mindset, who are working hard at leveraging and who are aware of how important it is to know all the players and the RIGHT people.

It short, the new comer most likely to get a mentor is one who is already working hard and helping himself and not looking for someone who can just smooth the way for him.

Chapter Number 3
Skills? Employment? Or Entrepreneur?
Sharing an Inspiring Story, I recently read

Sharing a Story
Quote "HIGHER EDUCATION - Does it really help?

Some town, Bengaluru is known the business hub of Bengaluru City with more than 1000 shops in the locality. This place is always crowed as people throng to buy clothes, furniture's, toys etc. at a wholesale price. Yesterday, I had been there as part of my educational research to talk to few shop keepers to understand how they do business and what education should do to them with regards to their business. During my interaction with many shop keepers in Some town, I found that, most of them were from Rajasthan. One more interesting thing that I found was that most of them were in their teenage. Out of all, meeting a young 10th dropout who runs a clothes shop was very interesting. His name is Entrepreneur from Rajasthan. I thought of sharing few our discussions here.

As I went into the crowded shop as a customer, he greeted me with a great smile calling "Anna banni, en bekithu". (Meaning: Brother, what do you want) (The conversation was in Kannada. I have translated it below)

Curious Me: I wanted to check for some nice shirt and pant piece.

Entrepreneur: Tell me sir, what is the range you are looking at?

Curious Me : You first show me all the clothes, let me choose out of those.

Entrepreneur: Sure, sir and started showing me all his collections. (Meanwhile during the selection time, I thought of asking him few questions, which was my only intention)

Curious Me : How did you learn Kannada?

Entrepreneur: Sir, obviously by talking to people.

Curious Me : But, your Kannada is very fluent!

Entrepreneur: Sir, initially, I found it difficult, but, when I continued speaking to customers, I learnt it on the fly. Now, I speak better than Bengaluru Kannadigas.

Curious Me : Superb. When did you start this business?

Entrepreneur: It's almost 10 years now. I started it when I failed in my 10th. My uncle got me into this business.

Curious Me : How many languages can you speak?

Entrepreneur: I can speak, Hindi, English, Kannada, Marathi, Tamil, Telugu & Malayalam.

Curious Me : Oh, my God ! How did you learn so many?

Entrepreneur: I told you sir, Customers taught me.

Curious Me : Sorry to ask you, but still out of curiosity, I just wanted to know what would be your monthly turnover?

Entrepreneur: Ummmm, it depends on the festival season. Normally, the turnover would be around 8 - 9 lakhs per month, and during festivals it will shoot up to 15 lakhs. Profit unto Rest. 4 lakhs per month.

Curious Me : What? Oh, my God! That's a super number! Great man!

Entrepreneur: What great sir? In Some town, this is very less. Others make double than what I do. Curious Me : Didn't you feel like completing your education by studying further?

Entrepreneur: Sir, to be honest, none of our family members completed education. To complete my education, it might take another 5 - 6 years which I feel is a big waste of time and money. I invested both in my business. Today, I will challenge none of the educated person with 10 year's experience will earn as much as I do. What do you say sir?

Curious Me : Hmmm....Yes. True. But still education would have helped you grow more than what you are earning today.

Entrepreneur: Seriously No sir. Education would give us fear and make us feel that, one should work under someone to earn their livelihood. Education does not teach us to live independently. I also have many friends who studied along with me and completed graduation. None are into business. Almost all are working in some private firm.

Curious Me : Hmmmm....So you don't regret completing education?

Entrepreneur: No sir. I am very happy. (In between our conversation, another customer had purchased around 20 pairs of shirt and pant, and few sarees. Without using a calculator Entrepreneur calculated the total cost of the purchase and told the customer the total cost including 10% discount in just 15 - 20 seconds).

Curious Me : Boss, you don't even use calculator?

Entrepreneur: Sir, educated people need calculator and mobile phones to calculate. Not me.

Curious Me : Started smiling and put my head down (because I was using calculator to calculate the cost of my purchase).

Entrepreneur: I continuously practiced calculating. I am doing this for 10 years and I have become perfect. I am sure, I will never err in my calculation.

After this, I made a purchase and the next whole day, I was thinking about our conversation again and again. I would like to infer what I learnt.

1. Without higher education, Entrepreneur is not jobless. Whereas our today's graduates with distinction are still in search of a job.

2. Without higher education, Entrepreneur has good communication skills. But, today's corporate world complains about our graduates for having no communication skills.

3. Without higher education, Entrepreneur earns in lakhs, whereas our current generation graduates complain of not having enough salary to pay their EMIs.

4. Without higher education, Entrepreneur's mathematical mind works faster than today's graduates who has cleared different levels of mathematics papers with high scores. Today's graduates need Mobile Phones to perform simple calculation.

5. Without higher education, Entrepreneur has no fear of losing his job, but today's graduate employees are always fear of getting fired from the company they are working in.
Now, the question in mind "HOW DOES HIGHER EDUCATION HELP ONESELF? POINT IS - SKILL DEVELOPMENT IS MORE VALUABLE THAN EDUCATION ! "End Quote.

Chapter Number 4

Own/Borrowed investment?
Self-Investment Tips

Self-Investment Tips that Work

It is true that time is the one commodity that most internet entrepreneurs have a very, very short supply of. Still there are ways to use time that would otherwise be of no value to invest in yourself. Here are a few tips that might help:

Use travel time to invest in yourself. By using your iPod or your MP3 player you can use your travel time to expand your knowledge.

Set your clock for a half hour earlier and use that time to read and learn.

After you stop working in the evening, use your computer to search for new information and ideas.

Of course, there are some things that are just going to take your time but you can choose wisely.

Attend webinars and tele-seminars that are directly related to your niche or your business.

Attend real world seminars that are closer to your home and will require less travel time but will provide you with the information that you need.

Resist the Urge of Staying in the Comfort Zone

We all have a comfort zone and all of us are very fond of our personal comfort zone. It is very, very tempting to just stick with doing the things that we have always done and doing them in the same way we have always done them.

However, staying in your comfort zone and refusing to expand your mind and your horizons can cause you and your internet business to fail.

There is an old saying (probably made up by someone who was afraid of trying new things) that says, "If it isn't broke, don't fix it." Well, 'it' doesn't have to be broken to be improved upon whatever 'it' is.

Candle light wasn't broken but we are all glad that electricity was harnessed. Electric light is still light but it is certainly a big improvement over candle light.

New ideas come along every day in the world of internet business. Some of those ideas are even good ones even if they do reside outside of our own personal comfort zone.

To continue to invest in yourself, you must be willing to leave your own comfort zone. Just because what has worked is still working it doesn't mean that there are not newer, better and more efficient ways of doing things.

Nobody is saying that new is always better. New is not always better but sometimes it is and the only way to tell which is which is by investigating new ideas yourself and then adapting the ones that can help you to your business.

Invest in yourself by increasing your knowledge and don't be afraid of trying new things and new ways of doing things. These things are the secrets of success and not just in the world of internet business but in life itself.

Chapter Number 5

You Like Work or Making Deals?
The Razor Edge Difference Between Work and Deals

Just about every internet marketer that I have ever known has worked at job other than internet marketing before they launched their internet marketing careers.

It is a funny thing about working at a job that pays you for the work that you do. You get into a 'work-equals- money' mindset. After all, when you work for others, work does, in fact, equal money.

But when you launch an internet marketing career the 'work' that used to make money for you now prevents you from making money.

It is true. The 'work' that you are doing that you once got paid to do, like answering the telephone, answering emails, filing papers, etc. is preventing you from making the deals that will put money in your pocket.

Yet we continue to seek work because we are programmed to think of work as the thing that makes money.

We get stuck in the 'work-equals-money' mindset that is counter-productive to building a successful internet marketing business.

We focus our time and energy on finding work for ourselves rather than on focusing our time and energy on making the deals that will make money for us.

It isn't hard to see why we get into this 'work-equals-money' mindset. We have been living with that concept since we were kids.

Think about it. What was your first job? Did you cut grass for a neighbor? Didn't you get money after you had done the work? Of course, you did. He wasn't paying you to think...he was paying you to cut grass.

When you got, older and got a job at the local burger joint, you got paid for cooking hamburgers and French Fries. You cooked the hamburgers and fries and then you got paid. Word did in fact equal money.

The owner of the hamburger joint wasn't paying you to find a better way to cook hamburgers or paying you to look for a new market to sell hamburgers. He was only paying you for doing the work of cooking the hamburgers.

But now you are not getting paid for doing the 'work'. The work isn't what is making money for you.

It is true that the work must still be done but you don't have to look for it. It will find you. What you need to be looking for now are the deals that will make you money.

What Constitutes Work?

What is 'work'? The 'work' that makes any business work is just the day to day activities that must be accomplished for the business to function. Telephone calls must be answered.

Emails must be read and responded to. Files must be kept orderly. The list goes on and on but this is just 'work'.

Nobody is going to pay you to answer the phone, read emails or keep files in order. That is simply 'work' that must be done. It isn't making you any money and it most certainly is not what you should be focused upon.

Once an internet marketing business has gotten up and running, it is a very good investment to simply pay a virtual assistant to do the 'work' and set yourself free to make the deals that make you money and make your internet marketing business thrive.

You can't do this right away, of course, but you can use as little of your time as possible on mundane tasks.

You can spend hours and hours and hours of your time working on your website.... making it better...tweaking this and tweaking that. That is work that is not putting a single red cent into your bank account.

Hire a techie to do that 'work' for you while you are making deals that make more than enough to pay the techie.

Until you can hire someone to do this work for you, get it fixed as best you can and move on the productive deal making.

How many hours are you spending each day writing and making posts to your blogs? Is this time making any money for you?

No, of course, it isn't. It is just 'work'. It is work that others could do just as well or work that you can find ways to make shorter like by using PLR materials rather than writing every word yourself.

Customer service is vital work that must be done. It must be done quickly and efficiently and above all competently.

It might even be work that in the beginning at least that you must do yourself.

There are however companies and individuals out there in cyber space that are perfectly capable of handling this work for you and you don't have to make it harder than it needs to be.

What Constitutes Making Deals?

Yes, it is true that the 'work' must be done, but the work that must be done should be done as quickly and as efficiently as possible and you shouldn't concentrate your energy on finding and creating more work that isn't going to making any money for you.

You need to be focusing your attention on making the deals that will make money.

Just as soon as you possibly can, you should begin to hire people to do the mundane tasks that must be accomplished and free up as much of your own time as possible for deal making.

So, what exactly are the activities that constitute deal making? Briefly and concisely they are the activities that have the potential for putting money into your bank account. A few of these activities are:

visiting forums and blogs that relate to your niche: Forums and blogs are where you find the real living, breathing people who are YOUR potential customers and until somebody drags out their credit card, puts in their information and buys products or services from you, you haven't made a dime so you need to go where the people are and find out how to best serve their wants and needs.

Visit websites that are related to your website. This is where you will find your potential joint venture partners. Contact the webmasters and work on making mutually profitable deals.

Start your own newsletter or E-zine: This is one of the most potentially profitable deals that you can make for yourself. The longer your list grows, the more profits you can make.

Attend seminars in the brick and mortar world and build good solid business relationships with others in your field. Here again are potential joint venture partners that you need to take the time to cultivate.

Put together your own webinar or tele-seminar: Find interesting speakers who would supply information of interest to your list. Webinars and tele-seminars are both easy and inexpensive to do and are both money making deals that you can make.

Does this Mean We Should Ditch Work and Focus on Entirely Deals Only?

It would be nice if we could just ditch the work-a-day-work and do nothing with our time other than make the deals that make us money! Now that would be what I would call a perfect world.

Unfortunately, the work-a-day-work must be done and until our 'ship comes in' we are probably going to be the ones who must do that as well as make the deals that make us money.

If we are going to have to do both we can at least learn how to work smarter. We can learn how to get the same amount of 'work' accomplished in less time so that we can free up more time for making the deals that will make us money.

Some examples of working smarter are:

Write a FAQ page for your website and use your autoresponder to direct most questions to that site.

Subscribe to a Private Label Rights (PLR) membership website and use that material (with only a little rewrite) as your blog posts and your website content. You can even make whole new products that can be sold from this PLR material.

Make a schedule for yourself that allows only so much time for the tasks that must be completed that make you no money and allow more time in that schedule for the deal making tasks that will make you money.

Invest in automation software that is designed to take care of simple every day but time consuming tasks.

There is always the 'work' that must be done every day but don't let it become the object of your focus. Don't look for work to be done. Work no longer equals money for you know that you are an internet marketer.

Get the work done as quickly as you can and put your focus on the deal making activities that will add to your bottom line. It is no longer your job just to make hamburgers...now you need to get out there and look for new markets. You ARE getting paid to think now.

Chapter Number 6

Why does your Startups need a Mentor?
How a Mentor helps?

An entrepreneur's life is tough and unpredictable. Often, you are faced with many doubts and challenges. At times, you even find yourself lurching from problem to problem! Against this backdrop, having a mentor or two on board your venture can benefit you tremendously.

A mentor is a priceless resource for any company, especially for companies that are in the startup stage. However, in India finding a good mentor is difficult. In fact, I'd even say that entrepreneurs in India can probably access funding more easily than they can find good mentors!

A good mentor can add enormous value to an enterprise. If an entrepreneur can benefit from mentoring, his/her chances of success (and the scale of success) are very likely to be higher than otherwise. At a nationwide level, therefore, we need thousands of very good mentors to support our booming base of entrepreneurs. This is true especially now, when the startup scene in India is seeing explosive action.

As an entrepreneur, you may be wondering: 'how exactly will a mentor add value to my company?'

Here is how.

He will hold a mirror to your business: A mentor will objectively assess the state of your business and the direction in which it is headed. He will bring in an unbiased point of view. In doing so, he will act as a mirror, reflecting the state of your business exactly as it is: warts, moles, blemishes and all. He will identify what's right and what's wrong with your business (or the business plan, depending on when exactly the mentor is brought on board) and help you fix things that need to be fixed.
If there is something wrong with the business (such as a weak process, poor

accounting standards, and a bad marketing plan, whatever) he will point it out to you and nudge you to take corrective action.

He will ask you tough questions: From time to time, the mentor acts as an examiner who poses tough questions to you, the entrepreneur. Not to needle and rattle you, but to get you thinking about improving things in your company. If the mentor does not perform this role diligently, complacency will most likely set in, giving you and yours team the feeling that all is well, when all may not be well.

A mentor's questions could pertain to the business model itself, the definition of target customers, the customer acquisition cost, the delivery times and SLAs, the time taken for the business to break-even, the extent of capital investment needed, the systems and processes being adopted, …. anything. For instance, I have seen mentors advise entrepreneurs to temporarily apply brakes on their efforts to develop the 'perfect' product and instead, go get their first set of paying customers.

He will make you step back: Because you have your nose to the grind always — operationally speaking — the mentor will pull you back a step every now and then, and make you see the big picture. He will help you look at the changes that are happening around you, which may have a bearing on your business. For instance, changes in consumer mindset, distribution channels, technology, law, etc. could all affect business and so, should be constantly factored into your planning.

He will open doors for you: As an entrepreneur, one of the biggest roadblocks you will face is a lack of professional contacts such as domain experts, service providers and potential employees. For instance, your business may need a website designer, an auditor, contacts in prospective client companies and an event manager, not to mention an investor. The mentor can make a few calls and put you in touch with the relevant agencies and people. It is up to you to take it from there.

He will push the bar higher: Entrepreneurs are often an unsure lot. While they want to make it big, deep down they are not sure if they will manage to achieve BIG goals. They are not sure how much to push themselves. A good mentor will demolish this self-doubt, instill large doses of confidence in the entrepreneur and make him push the bar high. As the saying goes, it is only when you aim for the stars that you will reach at least the moon.

He will share his value system with you: A good value system and work ethic are most important to a fledgling organization. If set up early, they can take the organization a long way. They help maintain a clean and healthy working environment. A mentor will share his professional value system with you and to the extent relevant, and get you to incorporate it in your organization.

He will motivate you and make you laugh: All the grind should be balanced with large doses of humor. A mentor with a sense of humor can indeed be a great asset to your business. His joie de vivre is likely to rub off on you and your team, with the result that all of you unwind occasionally and keep celebrating successes along the way. You will even learn to laugh hysterically at your mistakes and move on. All this eases the working atmosphere tremendously and helps you retain your sanity.

The mentor will also pat you on the back occasionally for a job well done or for a milestone achieved, thereby egging you on further.

He will teach your patience: The quest for success and for greatness is often long. You should weather many a storm and keep digging deeper into your reserves of strength, creativity and resilience. A mentor's sagacity will prove invaluable at such times. He will urge you not to fret (which is anyway useless), but to keep chipping away patiently.

The mentor has a big role to play in calibrating your tempo, curbing your impatience and helping you keep the faith.

In sum, a good mentor keeps his cross-hairs firmly on the interests of the business and from time to time, gives you the necessary inputs. And so, if you haven't brought a mentor or two on board your company yet, do it right away!

(In referring to mentors, I have used the masculine gender merely for ease of writing and not because of a gender bias!)

Chapter Number 7

Startup Founder vs Entrepreneur
Differences in Goals

What makes an entrepreneur different from a startup founder? Both individuals are investing in a company, but one will have more responsibility from another. A startup founder is completely different from an entrepreneur.

Who is an Entrepreneur?

An entrepreneur is an individual that looks for business opportunities and creates ways to make those businesses become profitable. Entrepreneurs often invest without the major responsibilities of running the companies as they focus more on earning money from them. Entrepreneurs try hard to create a viable business, not one that has a vague hope of succeeding. There are entrepreneurs all over the world. Even in poor areas of the world, people are entrepreneurs as they sell or trade goods to survive.

Who is a Startup Founder?

A startup founder is different from entrepreneurs as they found a startup company. They create a business that will someday become successful. While they sound like the entrepreneur, their goal is different. Unlike an entrepreneur, a startup founder doesn't have a major financial motive. They create a product or a service to change the world. They want to become famous or show others that anything is possible. While there can be a major payday in the future, they do not start off with the goal to make millions.

Differences in Goals

Both individuals need to have a strong personal drive to become successful. If you lack discipline and the ability to work hard, you can find yourself struggling to succeed. With an entrepreneurship, it is vital to create a product and be paid for it. Startup founders often do not worry about the selling process at first as they want to generate larger profits in the future. They go out and approach larger investors and focus on getting their business known. Depending upon the nature of your business, you can become successful online without every making a sale. Utilizing social media and other sites to become popular can help your business to become valuable to a major company or investor, and they will approach you about purchasing the business.

Which one is the best?

There are pros and cons for both areas. An entrepreneur may find himself out of money quickly if the sales are not coming in. They need to have financial backing for the first year or longer as they need to invest money into equipment, employees, and others to start generating products to sell. Some entrepreneurs will work upwards of 80 hours a week just to keep their company afloat.

A startup founder usually doesn't need to deal with all the financial day-to-day ongoing of the business. However, a startup founder takes a major risk by tying themselves to the company. Their reputation is at stake as they approach others and start marketing the business. If the business fails, the startup founder can lose everything. Their reputation can be destroyed, and it can take years to repair. Some startups will run for several years before they start to create an identity and make money.

Look at your financial situation, personal drive, and motivation, to determine if you have what it takes to become successful as a startup founder or entrepreneur.

Chapter Number 8
How I became a Mentor?
What No One Tells You About Seeking a Mentor for Your Startup I

I launched my first startup while I was still in school, 52 years ago. It shut up shop soon after. I then kept trying my hand at part time jobs, selling on commission basis, learnt to do odd/ menial job (there was no concept of child labor in my time and we had dignity in labor - there was no shame) just as the home climate was supportive especially after I lost my father when I turned 12.

At my uncle's place my aunts kept trying many small businesses - one was Divyang - a differently abled person and focused on knitting sweaters and woolen things from Kids to adults. We bought her a Knitting machine and soon she had orders from nearby novelty and fashion stores. She broke even and labored hard.

My other aunt was dynamic and socially very active. She bought a Potato chips/ wafers making machine - (we still had to deep fry them) and help her with weighing and packaging apart from visiting various sweetshops / Bars and restaurants to sell them and later collect the outstanding amounts.

I launched my second venture in 1993 and my sixth, in 1994. They also shut down within one year of launch and I was facing near bankruptcy. I sold all my assets, Apartment, Car, Mobile, Bikes, Pagers and Office Equipment and paid off my debtors and was lucky to make a clean Exit with a small INR 30k loan from a friend whom I paid off soon.

I could blame these failures on my naiveté and the fact that there wasn't much of a startup ecosystem to offer guidance and inspiration back then. But I should also blame myself, because if there was one thing I could have done differently, it would have been to get expert advice and insight from people far more successful than I.

If only I had had mentors back, then.

Flash forward to the present: I started my Seventh, and current, startup in 2012 with mentorship this time. I became a Mentor, Guide, Teacher, Philosopher, Pro-Bono Advisor, Blogger, Author, Artist, Professor and began Pro-Bono - Not for Profit Advisory. I did a couple of consulting assignments which kept me afloat but I had learnt that Mentoring is always FREE. To date, I have followed it. And throughout my journey, I've continued to reach out to experts from different domains for guidance and advice. From the experience, I've accrued in working with these mentors and my mentees, mentoring these startup entrepreneurs myself, I've realized this is something you can't do without. You need experts to help you with insights and with options that best resolve your challenges.

One of the main reasons for accelerator programs such as Y Combinatory or 500 Startups is the access they give to mentors and experts from different areas of business.

But when you do search for a mentor, there are several things to keep in mind, to make the best use of your mentor's time and build relationships with the right people who can help your startup grow. Here are three:

1. Know what you want from your mentor.

Why do you need a mentor at the current stage you're in? Do you need help with something specific, or are you looking for validation of your idea? Seeking out mentors for idea validation is the single biggest mistake most startup founders make. I personally get five to eight emails every day from people asking what I think of their idea and whether I have any feedback. Two things here:

The mentor/person you're writing to may not be your potential target audience for the product. The idea should be validated by your potential customers. If you can get someone to pay to use your product, there's your validation.
Most ideas (if they don't already exist) seem outrageous or weird, at first. Most of the "experts" and investors who initially reviewed the concept of Twitter rejected it. After all, (they must have thought), who needs a 140-

character texting vehicle?

So, don't worry about your idea's radical differences. Instead, look for a mentor for the correct reason: help with a specific aspect/challenge of your business.

2. Mentors should be experts, not generalists.

With that said, your mentors ideally should be experts in your industry, able to resolve the issues you're facing. Don't seek generalists, like startup founders, who are likely to give general advice.

You typically don't need general startup advice because your product/service, market, customers and situation all differ from those of from other entrepreneurs. Instead, seek out those mentors who are the experts. For instance, if you realize that you've been spending a great deal of money advertising on Facebook without getting good returns, seek out that expert in Facebook or paid advertising who can best guide and coach you in leveraging this medium (along with other options).

3. Be creative when asking someone to be a mentor

Most people who are successful in their areas of expertise are inundated with emails from people asking for feedback or advice. So, you need to stand out and to be creative in your outreach.

When one encounters challenges with SEO in business, one reaches out to the best SEO experts in the world, albeit in a creative manner: One sets up an expert advice platform for entrepreneurs who, like you, had queries with regards to specific areas of marketing. You go out and interview those experts and put their advice out as videos for a larger audience.

You benefit from such action, as have many startup entrepreneurs with similar problems. So, follow this example: Be creative in how you reach out or build a relationship, by following experts' blogs, commenting on their articles, retweeting their articles (by tagging them) and engaging with them on social media. Add value to their work before you expect something back.

And, then, shoot off an email to them with a specific query. Don't write asking for general advice.

Finally, don't expect mentors to give you an hour of their time every week or, heaven forbid, every day, for your business. Consider these people sounding boards for the challenges you face or the specific ideas you want to bounce around. Mentors should be catalysts for your personal and professional growth. Just make sure you're not asking too much of them.

www.ingramcontent.com/pod-product-compliance
Lightning Source LLC
Chambersburg PA
CBHW051110180526
45172CB00002B/855